THE ENGLISH ASSOCIATION

Presidential Address
1947

THE NOVELS OF
GEORGE MEREDITH
AND SOME NOTES ON THE
ENGLISH NOVEL

BY

SIR OSBERT SITWELL
Bart., LL.D.

November 1947

THE NOVELS OF GEORGE MEREDITH AND SOME NOTES ON THE ENGLISH NOVEL

IT has been well said that if a thing is worth doing at all, it is worth doing badly: yet I feel some hesitation in addressing this audience to-day; and for more than one reason. Vain as I may be in all else, I have never considered myself even as competent to lecture, and criticism I have ever eschewed. My plight is all the worse because we have in the chair to-day Mr. Charles Morgan, who, apart from his great creative gifts, has in the course of the last few years proved himself to be the most interesting of critics of modern literature, a *creative* critic, a diviner of life, and a friend to beauty wherever he sees it.

Why, then, I may well ask myself, have I chosen a writer so august as Meredith, on whom to descant before so select a gathering? . . . For several reasons: but chiefly for this; that it would be possible for even this great novelist, laureate of the later Victorian novelists, to go farther and fare worse. Because, for some years past, indifferent writers have been at pains to ransack, not only the library-shelves, but even the waste-paper baskets of Great Britain, to find earlier authors about whom to write. By their aid has many a pygmy been expanded to the stature of a giant, only to burst before the last page, like a toy balloon outstretched in the blowing by a child. Others, unable to find a suitable drug-addict or too weak to drag the body of some very minor poet from the asylum cemetery, have fallen upon the corpses of the really great. But, singularly, while the puny and the warped, of never fully developed gifts, have been extolled, equally the giant has been degraded, or, in the pretty idiom of our day, debunked, to be shown to the reader as another dwarf or deformity. It is odd, therefore, that George Meredith should so far have escaped the attentions of the body-snatchers, and should have been left in peace in the unfashionable seclusion of the grave. We must, in consequence, continue to hope that so great a writer may, when he comes once more to be written about, fall into the hands of some critic who has the right to appraise him, and may be spared the nibbling of the unworthy. For, though prophecy is a more dangerous calling even than criticism, let me, as an oracle, make a sole prognostication in the world of literature: before long we shall be given more than one life of Meredith, together with many briefer comments on his achievement. And, in the same way that shortly after the success of John Drinkwater's *Abraham Lincoln*, Bernard Shaw, when asked why he had chosen to write about St. Joan, is said to have replied, 'To save her from Drinkwater', so I make these few comments in an effort to prevent Meredith falling into other hands: since I cherish a great love for him.

I must, in the first place, make it plain that I regard him as a great English novelist, and before proceeding to detail, declare that I am here making no attempt to evaluate his worth in his other literary personality, as a famous poet. Concerning my authority to judge him as a novelist, I may urge a frequent reading of the majority of his books. I began to read him, I think out of a sort of highbrow snobbery, when I was very young—far too young to understand him: I believe I was twelve. Probably I should have been then happier still with such novels of adventure as those of Robert Louis Stevenson—but I was *not* too young to feel, as I finished one of Meredith's books, in how heightened a world of experience I had been plunged. *The Egoist, The Ordeal of Richard Feverel,* and *Evan Harrington* I have read and re-read many times, some I know less well, one or two, the *Shaving of Shagpat,* for instance, not at all. Lately I have read again as many as I could obtain; but these great novels in our barbarous times are out of print, and so I have only re-read *The Egoist, Evan Harrington, The Amazing Marriage, One of Our Conquerors, Lord Ormont and his Aminta,* and *Rhoda Fleming.* Yet I hope you will not consider me too ill-qualified to discuss him as writer. When a critic—and such, I must to-day pretend to be—states that any author is a *great* novelist, he should always be invited to state whom else he considers to be in the same category: otherwise how is it possible for the audience to test the range of his critical faculties, or even to apply any calliper to his meanings? So let me, while confining myself to the limits of the nineteenth century, proclaim certain allegiances. Unpatriotically, I must confess that to me the greatest novelists of Meredith's epoch, or of any other, are the French novelists, Stendhal, Balzac, Flaubert, Maupassant: the greatest English novelist of the period, because of the whole and fantastic world to which he gave life, Dickens. Meredith, albeit so much more of a conscious artist than was Dickens, did not create people in the same way, like a god. On the contrary, he left a record of a section of a world which others knew. In the creation of character he is not equal to—not a tenth of an equal of—Dickens, and when not seldom he attempts—as we will see in a moment—the sort of character whom Dickens would have evolved so easily and imbued so distinctively with life, the difference is very plain. But Meredith is also something which Dickens is not, except by the occasional accident of his genius; Meredith is a great stylist.

Now style can be a worldly—I almost said wordy—misfortune to an author; nothing so immensely, so frequently, so inescapably comes between him and his public. But, to the contrary, it was Meredith's style which—quite justly—won him in his lifetime adherents for his works. Though on occasion the reader was obliged to read a sentence three or four times to obtain its full drift and implication, he was somehow persuaded not to mind that—but, of course, this quality of Meredith's limited his flock in number. It is a peculiar paradox that whereas a style prevents an author from obtaining for his novel when it at first appears the widest democratic popularity, yet no good novel—unless it be the work of a raging genius such as Dickens—can continue to exist after his death unless it possess this nearly indefinable and very protean quality. Obversely, bad style exists as well as good, and it is the solvent of a bad style which almost magically produces at once for certain novels two million readers: even a title, as with *Forever Amber*, can be redolent of style. But a bad style kills the novel of this kind, directly its day is over, whereas a good style preserves a book, and if a novelist wishes for his work to live in terms of centuries, rather than of years, he must somehow contrive to infuse it thus with his own personality, though he must never himself step down into one of his books. . . . Unfortunately, English novelists, myself included, are apt to allow themselves to get in the way (Mr. Charles Morgan is an exception), to step in and talk about their characters, instead of letting the characters talk for themselves: it is a very real temptation to us. And when Meredith struts in the arena, or rather from a cloud addresses his flock directly, he is particularly irritating because of the languid, unbiased, philosophical attitude of laughing-in-his-sleeve, which he coyly assumes.

All authors, good or bad, are—I speak generally—equal in one respect after their death; for a decade or two they are unreadable. The majority of readers are by then in reaction against the age, the decade, the year, of which the author was the embodiment. Then, if the author is a good writer, the tide turns, and the faithful reveal themselves, and more are added to their numbers. Thus Meredith is plainly now readable again. His style revivifies his characters, though the circumstances out of which they and their problems grew, and the manner in which they lived, have perished utterly. Even when Meredith does not directly describe it, even when, as in *Sandra Belloni*, he is treating of the impact of an Italian artiste upon the aspiring members of the family of a city merchant, or as in *One of Our Conquerors* of a magnate who dreams of Respectability and a house in Leatherhead, yet the novelist's ideal world—that which he upholds in his heart as a secret standard, and against which, as he weighs it, all others are found wanting—is the world of the former English Artificial Paradise, the Country-House. And in Meredith's novels, very artificial and fascinating it is!

In days when in English literature, as in English life, the public-house has replaced the country-house as an ideal, those readers who like country-houses are suspect: yet the background of the country-house is certainly one against the stately processes of which action is displayed to advantage. Moreover, with some of the fiction-writers of to-day, popular and typical in their generation, who explain the psychology of lunatics in asylums, probably the background is the very same as in Meredith's novels, for the homes of the Feverels and the Patternes will have been sold by now and have been converted into lunatic asylums, and this, I hope, may in the end endear them to left-wing critics. In any case, I allege that in Meredith's novels the country-house supplies a very fascinating background. Nor can I personally be accused of prejudice in the matter, for I have always bitterly hated the existence led in any country-house but my own—and that, in its life, resembles no other, being, in so far as I can make it such, a place of seclusion in which to work.

The real country-house was a place where bored but very healthy men could just get through life with the aid of estate work, port wine, and rural pursuits. The owner would tire himself out in the hunting-field, and at night fall into a slumber, faster and more long-continued than any that a drug could induce. (In parentheses we may notice that the difference in class which distinguishes the worlds of Dickens and Meredith is typified by the alcohol consumed in their pages; hardly a book of Meredith's exists in which port, that deadly nectar of the gentry, does not make its appearance: whereas throughout Dickens's novels is exhaled the more vulgar enticing aroma of hot punch.) Sportsmen used, in fact, to kill such golden days as Meredith described. How exquisitely he describes them, how easy it is, even, from this distance, to feel at home in those airy vistas, partly concealed by a golden mist: yet it must be remembered that there is always in them something delusive, the flavour of an ideal; the fantastic Ideal of the Country-House which Meredith invented for himself, and cherished, because it was so removed from his own origin, and from the tainting shadow of his grandfather, old Mel, Mr. Snip, the Portsmouth tailor, who comes to life so magnificently in the pages of *Evan Harrington*!

It has been in this connexion, at times, the vogue to call Meredith a snob. It is no more snobbish, I believe, to place ultimate credence in the country-house than in the public-house or the doss-house, in a duke, than in a grab-and-run bandit or a charwoman, no more boastful to brag of long descent than of short. To the novelist, as to his creator, there is no class, no individual, that is not of *vital* interest: for him in this, unlike the politician, the human being who is not worth a tinker's cuss—or, in a more elegant simile, two hoots—does not exist. But the being must be alive. The country-house of Meredith, full of relatives and echoing vastly with an Augustan life, is as much of a convention as the so different imaginary country-houses of Meredith's father-in-law, Thomas Love Peacock, or the miner's cottage, throbbing with physical love, of D. H. Lawrence. I think Meredith genuinely loved an aristocrat: he liked the robust speech of the great Victorian ladies, so different to the caged-in, mincing ways of the contemporary bourgeoisie, he liked the pride and generosity of the men: their swift return to old habits, their inclination to fight duels, and the facilities offered them by Club Steps for public horse-whippings: opportunities of which contemporary novelists took full advantage. Further, some of that which may appear to the censorious to be snobbery is merely the effect of a change in habits and morals. To become obsolete—of which quaintness, so termed, is the first symptom—makes for absurdity. As a bird, the dodo is ridiculous—as the Ancient Briton, woaded and wielding a club, is a comic figure—merely because he is dead. Even the moral problems with which Meredith deals, the illnesses he describes, have disappeared or become transformed beyond recognition. Within a decade of his death, the entire ideal world of the novel had changed utterly. In Meredith's books to appear in a divorce court would have meant the ruin of a man, still more of a woman: by the time Wells was writing his Edwardian novels the whole tone had altered, and an appearance in the divorce court had almost taken the place of a presentation at Court in Queen Victoria's day. . . . Since then, things have changed more rapidly. The horse-whip—together with the horse—has disappeared. Brain-fever no longer exists as the complete solution for novelists when in a tight corner with a character. (It is now called meningitis, but is not used in this way.) In *The Ordeal of Richard Feverel*, for example, both hero and heroine have brain-fever. In *Rhoda Fleming*, Rhoda's sister Dahlia has it, and if I remember correctly, there are sufferers from it, too, in *One of Our Conquerors*. Even the ladies with slightly damaged reputations, bold and brave but contaminating, the ladies who were not received in the great world, and whom he so brilliantly describes, have, like the great world itself, ceased to exist. Yet in spite of the obsolete tricks Meredith practised, his novels will find, I prophesy, an increasing public in the course of the next ten years.

I have ever been a plodder, not a skipper, with books. When first as a small boy I read this great novelist, I seem to remember that at times I was profoundly bored—though I would not admit it to myself—until, all at once, the atmosphere had taken me captive. . . . In that remarkable autobiography, *The Education of Henry Adams*, the author has a passage describing how, after attending many concerts in Berlin, and not in the least enjoying them; how, then, suddenly his defences collapsed, and music—I think it was the work of Beethoven—took him captive: henceforward concerts became his chief pleasure. It is a similar process with the persistent reader of Meredith. After a period that seems to him tedious, he will find himself swimming with the stream, and immensely enjoying the physical sensations of it. Directly you open one of this famous author's novels, you are again in a land bathed in the golden light and mist produced by his style—a prospect at once recognizable, spacious, with great stretches of undulating country, broken up by moral boundaries solid as stone walls and plain for all to see. Now, to-day, the stones have crumbled, the boundaries have merged, and this may make it a difficult landscape at first for the young to appreciate. But it is a country full of ennobling love, and one where the human relationships revealed have a peculiar value never quite to be assessed to the full extent. Nevertheless, it is a world as remote from ours as that described by Lady Murasaki in *Tales of Genghi*. It may even seem strange to the young that there are persons in this room to-day who lived in that civilization of *The Egoist* or *Diana of the Crossways*. I read of it myself in these novels, just after it was over: for it was essentially Victorian, and I began to read Meredith about 1906. To-day, it is a prospect indeed difficult to identify, but none the less fascinating. Its vistas are tranquil, for all its alleged excitements, the avenues are formal, in spite of the peculiar mists which cling to the trees. Everybody is in his or her place, the workman happy grumbling in his cottage, the landlord arrogantly at ease in his castle, the fallen woman almost joyously aware of her degradation, the gallant soldier, armed with his horse-whip, ready to strike—but all for the moment made of genuine flesh and blood. Who is to recognize this world, now that the poor man finds a communal home in the rich man's castle, while the rich man crouches at his gate or lives in the mews, and now that, like almost everything else, the horse-whip is, as they say in the shops, in short supply? In this obsolete world a very high standard of conduct prevails—and of chivalry, to-day absolutely defunct. Nevertheless, the apparent improbability, from the viewpoint of the present, of the action of his books, the non-existence in the modern state of the types he portrays in them, in no manner mars their authenticity. They continue to exist on their own plane, as works of art. The aroma of them, their fragrance, permeates the air while you read. Their beauty, their wisdom, reside in their style and atmosphere, comparable to those of a great picture. Without his superb mastery of paint, and delight in it, the later pictures of Titian—such as the *Tarquin and Lucretia* in Vienna—might be clearer, more defined, but they would have lost their unique interest.

Nor is it, I think, that the stories Meredith tells, the plots he invents, are of consuming interest: they do not compare with the rich improbability and inventive delights of Dickens, they have none of the doomed inevitability of Thomas Hardy's masterpieces. The stories are plain, and in the same fashion as the characters, extinct. No, for their effect they depend upon the emotions engendered in our hearts by the figures gesticulating through the haze, illuminated and illuminating. We have, until we are deep in the books, lost the key to what they signal; some of it we can never decipher, but the *emotion* remains, the love, the hatred, the pity—all these emanate as strongly as ever from the pages! Surely no love-scenes in the world are more poignant than those which deal with Richard Feverel and his young Lucy Desborough at the water's edge, among the rushes, nothing can be more pitiful than his later separation from her. The characters, some of them at times platitudinously drawn and inclined to be stereotyped, move now, to-day, in a vacuum: in consequence they offer an abstract pattern, and are, for that, the more fascinating to watch. But emotion, strong as the scent of wood or mountain, still comes up from the words. There is nothing artificial about the loves and hatreds and jealousies—even though the story may seem artificial—for Meredith was a great writer. And further, to revert once more to Titian, just as his figures are more portentous because of their nebulosity (though there is nothing *uncertain* about them), so, too, the beings who emerge from the hazy radiance of Meredith's prose, their bodies dripping with golden light and passing from sun to shadow with a mastery of chiaroscuro, are all the more solid in themselves for the mist which surrounds them.

The humour—the delightful humour—of Meredith exists in the drawing of his characters, and in the situations. It is not, I hold, verbal. His vaunted wit, as stylized as it is celebrated, seems to me the very opposite of his humour, and often to be deplorable. It *sounds* funny without *being* funny: the most tedious trait that alleged wit can show. How tired one grows of Mrs. Mountstuart Jenkinson's label for Sir Willoughby Patterne, 'He has a leg'! It becomes unbearable, means nothing, falls empty off the tongue. Yet it does not make the reader impatient of the book. *The Egoist* remains a monument of English fiction. If not the wit, the humour is superb: so is the irony. *Evan Harrington* is a great humorous novel, the Countess de Saldar in it, a superb and truthful comic creation. Strangely, Meredith is comparable to an author so different from him as Dickens, in that his humour is best when *richly* comic, as in the study of Mr. Pericles in *Sandra Belloni*, and also in his creation of lesser characters, such as Richard Feverel's great-aunt, known as 'The Eighteenth Century'. Here one is enabled almost to catch the very tones of the long, digestive conversations that take place after dinner between the old lady and her valetudinarian nephew Hippias. The opulence of Meredith's invention, and the fineness of his aesthetic quality, is shown in the singular ease with which he is able to swing off aphorisms for Sir Austin Feverel, epigrams good enough to fill the page by themselves, but always in style, and so typical of the character the novelist portrays that they are irresistibly comic and tragic. How greatly does one come to look forward to the casual introduction of one of these apophthegms from the Pilgrim's inexhaustible *Scrip*! Similarly, when the novelist chooses to introduce a poem by a character, it is always good in itself, absolutely true to its supposed creator in the book, and I can think of no other great story-teller so successful in this respect.

The Italian innocence of Sandra Belloni exhibits another incidental virtue and ability of Meredith's; the way in which, without any feeling of patronage, he can seize on national character and expose it. *Sandra* is in her essence Italian. Dickens, on the other hand, though he loved France, and enjoyed life in Paris more than in London, could never create a foreign, least of all a French, character. If a villain was wanted, as the devilish scoundrel with whom the book opens in *Little Dorritt*, or Lady Dedlock's maid in *Bleak House*, the fact that he or she is French at once accounts, without any other motive having to be produced, or any other explanation having to be given, for the iniquitous behaviour and exploits of the character in question. This attitude, I take it, was a legacy to the common man from the Napoleonic Wars. Also, of course, the English were at the zenith of their power, and believed all foreigners to be children, ridiculous and unreasoning. But this was *not* the case with Meredith, who had been educated for some years at a school abroad, and was a European as well as an Englishman. His talent approached genius: whereas Dickens, possessed of so many and so much greater faults, was, of course, a genius without any qualifications being attached to the term. But Meredith's foreigners are among the best in English fiction, far better than those of Dickens; and even when shown to be ridiculous, as with Mr. Pericles, the amateur of opera, in *Sandra Belloni*, that is because, like certain Englishmen, they *are* ludicrous, not because they are foreigners.

On the other hand, Dickens's superiority in certain respects is manifest. If we take the character of Skepsey, the boxing patriotic clerk to Mr. Victor Radnor, in *One of Our Conquerors*, a great weakness is evident when compared to any similar creation of Dickens. For Skepsey is—or could be —a Dickens character: though it may also be argued that he is merely a character in the English tradition, which Dickens and Meredith both inherited. Dickens, albeit a fondness for labels often betrays even him, could manage that particular *genre* better than any other English novelist. When a broad comic character enters, it is true that we know what to expect: Weller will tiresomely clip his w's, Tapley will give the V-sign as often as Winston Churchill in the war, and generally be as cheerful as Mr. Shinwell before a new coal crisis, Mrs. Gamp will want her rum; but of whatever kind the patent, the hall-mark, we are obliged, even sometimes against our will, to shout our appreciation: whereas Meredith's Skepsey always a little lets us down, we close the fresh chapter of each of his appearances disappointed anew. And even his creator seems too bored with him, as the book goes on, to give us much about his third appearance in the witness-box. Again, Dickens often bestows upon his comic characters names which tax the credulity of a reader: he gets away with it, by the particular power of his genius. But while Dickens himself never inflicted upon his readers so palpable a comic invention as the name *Mrs. Chump* for one of the farcical characters in *Sandra Belloni*, yet, in a broad way, she is funny, in spite of the manner in which the author, by thus christening her, has sacrificed our sympathy.

Apropos of Mrs. Chump in *Sandra Belloni*, however, there is one thing difficult to comprehend. I may have misunderstood this novel, but the author seems to me to regard and to treat Mrs. Chump's ruin, as a result of Mr. Pole heartlessly gambling away her funds—of which he is trustee— while making love to her in order to keep her quiet, with an unbecoming levity; especially unbecoming, that is to say, in a Great Victorian, so Trust-Fund-Conscious. I can only imagine that the contempt he showed for his public in christening a character Mrs. Chump led him too in the end to despise her unduly. If Dickens had created a similar person and situation, he would have extracted every inch of pathos, and even perhaps of tragedy, out of poor Mrs. Chump. . . . Yet, let us admit, *Sandra Belloni* is a novel great of its kind. Sandra Belloni herself is exquisite, and the whole atmosphere of Brookfield remains memorable for its pretentiousness; while the garden party at Besworth Lawn, under the patronage of Lady Gosstree, provides a situation which Marcel Proust would have loved to exploit, and which indeed, shows something, not, it is true, of his style, but of his treatment. I wonder if Proust ever read Meredith. He certainly read both Dickens and Ruskin.

To revert to our earlier comparison, Meredith's actual jokes are not as good as those of Dickens. On this matter I only dwell because the claim must be made for him that he is a great writer of comedy as well as of tragedy. He saw himself as the particular exponent of the Comic Spirit. But the jokes of the Victorian writers are apt to be in inverse ratio to their greatness as Victorians. Samuel Butler, in his own way great, is not a great Victorian in the sense that Meredith or Tennyson were great Victorians: but he is a much wittier writer than Meredith, though scarcely a more successful novelist. And, so much did Butler write ahead of his time that it never fails to surprise us to realize that he was writing and making notes for *The Way of All Flesh*, that superb monument of satire and irony, in the seventies, at the same time Meredith was at work on one of his greatest novels, in a way similar in theme, yet how different in feeling, *The Egoist*. Apropos of these two men, it is also interesting to recall that Meredith, when reader for Messrs. Chapman & Hall, refused Butler's *Erewhon* with the curt comment '*will not do*'. But, to return to what I was saying, Meredith's chief characters are noble, not pitiable—though they can be detestable: it is the lesser creations who often provide the chief delights of his novels. The heroes and heroines often confound us with their virtues and failings. Such heroes as the boxing schoolmaster, Matey Weyburn, in *Lord Ormont and his Aminta*, who begins life as a model school-boy and ends as a model master, thereby combining the worst possible of both worlds, is quite as mawkish as the most fragrant of Dickens heroines. . . . Consider, for a moment, how Butler would have exhibited such a character to us! But then, while possessing a fantastic and ingenious mind, Butler was very suspicious, almost morbidly apprehensive of possible moral or aesthetic imposture. Like the Dowager—of whom Cocteau tells us in one of his books—who declared and genuinely believed that Stravinsky's *Sacre du Printemps* had been written and produced to pull her leg, so Butler appears to have held that Darwin had developed his theory merely in order to bait him, and that the whole of music, after the time of Handel, had been composed to make mock of him. Remarkable as were his gifts, he remains in essence an unattractively familiar person, the *Embattled Philistine*. That, Meredith never was! He did not deal in ideas, he scarcely questioned accepted beliefs, his tragedies sometimes verge on Drawing-Room Tragedy—though he often transcended those boundaries—but he was never afraid of other people. The great novelist never allowed himself for a moment to be influenced by the critics. He was sure of his own way. He did not mind if he was thought obscure, over-stylized, affected, impersonal—or if he minded it, he did not allow it to deflect him from his course. . . . But Butler was afraid—afraid, not so much of the critics, whom he had taught himself to despise, as of the great Victorians; was Darwin trying to pull a fast one over him? did Pater take him for a mug? —such, in the parlance of a later day, were the questions he asked himself. Never for a single instant would they have troubled Meredith.

Somewhere in his note-books—that admirable collection—Butler remarks that the prose style of Walter Pater reminds him of the Cherry Blossom Face Powder on the countenance of Madame Rachel. For a long time I thought the satirist was referring to the great actress described so movingly in Charlotte Brontë's *Villette*, but after reading recently a book devoted to notorious Victorian characters, I perceive that it must have been a more topical allusion—to the disreputable Madame Rachel of Bond Street who ran one of the first beauty-parlours, and was involved in several unsavoury lawsuits. It was a criticism which might have applied equally to the prose-style of George Meredith. The style is thick, inspissated, at times perfumed, so that we wish occasionally that it were clearer, but only in the same way we might wish the same thing of a painting by Tintoretto or Titian. What sort of a world is it that he has so plainly revealed, and yet so earnestly obscured? . . . Its chief feeling, I think, is one of predestination—not the tragic and superb sense of predestination which pervades the novels of Hardy, such as *Tess of the D'Urbervilles* or *Jude the Obscure*, books governed by a belief so strong that it makes all illusion credible, that we are creatures of the earth, yet with souls struggling through a dark fog to an end that in its tragedy ennobles even such perverse and pitiful creatures as we may seem to be. No, in Meredith's world, mortals, physically at ease in their surroundings—a fact which leads them to believe that they can follow their own lines of action—march towards a reasonable goal. Yet their slow progress entails a struggle within the beautiful mesh of gold and silver their creator provides for them, while the gods continue, without our ever being able to pierce through the haze to their purpose, to dictate a policy of Unconditional Surrender from their country-seat on Mount Olympus. Yet, in spite of its haziness, and its disasters, the earth below—earth is too earthy a term—is a prosperous and civilized place. With Hardy's novels, the reader exclaims, '*This* is the world: every man ends like this!' With Meredith's, 'This is a warning: it might happen, but in any case it would be a rare event!'

Noticeable, too, is it how Meredith himself peers down through the luteous mist of his own creation, like a god, implying, by what he says, the sentiment, 'This is how it happened to the poor playthings of my confrères on Mount Olympus', or, like the sun, he shows us mountain and valley, but does not explain them. When, however, Meredith does condescend to step down into his own work, even then, he never explains, but, instead, philosophizes with, if the truth is to be told, an airy tedium. Notwithstanding his assumption of an Olympian manner, the reader nevertheless accepts the validity and the conventions of his world. Never does he seek to oppose the author, as well he might, with 'It never could happen', or 'It never did happen': *never*, albeit every single one of his novels, from having been true to the conditions of the time and to the conventions of the class for which he wrote, has become, in its very existence, artificial; absolutely artificial. Every assumption of every character, the very right he takes for granted to be where he is, on his cloud, has since been challenged and overthrown. The literary world is now under the spell of a very different ideal from that which existed as a convention in the novels of the nineteenth century. The old Byronic hero of the early years, the baronet of Meredith, the aesthete of Oscar Wilde, has been superseded by the Little Man, disagreeably placid under the bombs: the delicate heroines have been ousted from their place by the charwoman, who as a heroine, to paraphrase Walter Pater on the Mona Lisa, is that which in the ways of a thousand years men have come to desire. D. H. Lawrence introduced the miner-hero, the game-keeper; and to-day the Little Man, smug child of a distracted age, has descended farther and become the inmate of an asylum. If my memory is not at fault Sir Max Beerbohm once showed a caricature of a connoisseur contemplating an African carving, under the heading:'We Needs must Love the Lowest when we See it'. Kafka, whose influence is so evident in the intelligent English and Continental fiction of the day, gave the last psychological twist to the Little-Man—Charwoman

Ideal, now grown as artificial, though in a different direction, as Meredith's baronet.

Perhaps you cannot call Meredith's baronets his *heroes*; but it is true that once a baronet enters the pages of one of his novels, he steals the limelight entirely. Yet I prefer the other baronets in other novels; the majestic stalking, for example, of Sir Leicester Dedlock in *Bleak House*, for he is presented with just that amount of distortion which makes for truth: whereas Meredith, although his characters exist in their own peculiar atmosphere, is a realist. Meredith's great world is less interesting to me than Dickens's occasional distortion of it, but far more interesting than Thackeray's footmen-infested pages: while Sir Leicester Dedlock's august reproofs to Miss Volumnia are to me as memorable as Sir Austin Feverel's epigrams. Let us recall Sir Leicester for a moment, talking to his middle-aged but girlish cousin about the General Election, in a condensed version.

'How are we getting on?' says Miss Volumnia, clasping her hands. 'Are we safe?'

'I regret to say, Volumnia, that in many places the people have shown a very bad spirit, and that this opposition to the Government has been of a most determined and implacable description.'

'W-r-retches,' says Volumnia.

'Even,' proceeds Sir Leicester glancing at the circumjacent cousins on sofas and ottomans, 'even in many—in fact in most of those places in which the Government has carried it against a faction—even in them, I am shocked, for the credit of Englishmen, to inform you that the Party has not triumphed without being put to enormous expense. Hundreds,' says Sir Leicester, eyeing the cousins with increasing dignity and swelling indignation, 'hundreds of thousands of pounds!'

If Volumnia have a fault, it is the fault of being a trifle too innocent; seeing that the innocence which would go extremely well with a sash and tucker, is a little out of keeping with the pearl necklace. Howbeit, impelled by innocence, she asks, 'What for?'

'Volumnia,' remonstrates Sir Leicester, with his utmost severity, 'Volumnia!'

'No, no, I don't mean what for,' cries Volumnia with her favourite little scream. 'How stupid I am! I mean what a pity!'

'I am glad,' Sir Leicester says, 'that you do mean what a pity!'

Meredith's baronets were never so majestic, nor so exaggeratedly life-like as *that*! Yet it would be incorrect if future generations were to conclude that Meredith's characters were untrue to life. These were baronets in the golden age of baronetcy, and Sir Willoughby and Sir Austin were archetypes of some whom I knew well, and saw frequently; true even down to the epigrams of *The Pilgrim's Scrip*.

In mentioning these two gentlemen, let me say that these two books, *The Ordeal of Richard Feverel* and *The Egoist*, seem to me immeasurably the greatest of Meredith's works, far greater than *Diana of the Crossways*. In them we find his gifts at their highest; his sense of character, and the interplay of one or another; many were his lesser masterpieces, *Sandra Belloni*, *Beauchamp's Career*, *Evan Harrington*, but these two stand alone, in their understanding, in the emotion they engender, in the romantic beauty they disclose. These books are true to all life, to human nature, and belong to no one period. Let us, to end this address, listen to the master as he describes Richard Feverel's first glimpse of Lucy by the water's edge:

When nature has made us ripe for love, it seldom occurs that the Fates are behindhand in furnishing a temple for the flame.

Above green-flashing plunges of a weir, and shaken by the thunder below, lilies, golden and white, were swaying at anchor among the reeds. Meadow-sweet hung from the banks thick with weed and trailing bramble, and there also hung a daughter of earth. Her face was shaded by a broad straw hat with a flexible brim that left her lips and chin in the sun, and, sometimes nodding, sent forth a light of promising eyes. Across her shoulders, and behind, flowed large loose curls, brown in shadow, almost golden where the ray touched them. She was simply dressed, befitting decency and the season. On a closer inspection you might see that her lips were stained. This blooming young person was regaling on dewberries. They grew between the bank and the water. Apparently she found the fruit abundant, for her hand was making pretty progress to her mouth. Fastidious youth, which revolts at woman plumping her exquisite proportions on bread-and-butter, and would (we must suppose) joyfully have her scraggy to have her poetical, can hardly object to dewberries. Indeed the act of eating them is dainty and induces musing. The dewberry is a sister to the lotus, and an innocent sister. You eat: mouth, eye, and hand are occupied, and the undrugged mind free to roam. And so it was with the damsel who knelt there. The little skylark went up above her, all song, to the smooth southern cloud lying along the blue: from a dewy copse dark over her nodding hat the blackbird fluted, calling to her with thrice mellow note: the kingfisher flashed emerald out of green osiers: a bow-winged heron travelled aloft, seeking solitude: a boat slipped toward her, containing a dreamy youth: and still she plucked the fruit, and ate, and mused, as if no fairy prince were invading her territories, and as if she wished not for one, or knew not her wishes. Surrounded by the green shaven meadows, the pastoral summer buzz, the weir-fall's thundering white, amid the breath and beauty of wild flowers, she was a bit of lovely human life in a fair setting; a terrible attraction. The Magnetic Youth leaned round to note his proximity to the weir-piles, and beheld the sweet vision. Stiller and stiller grew nature, as at the meeting of two electric clouds. Her posture was so graceful, that though he was making straight for the weir, he dared not dip a scull. Just then one enticing dewberry caught her eyes. He was floating by unheeded, and saw that her hand stretched low, and could not gather what it sought. A stroke from his right brought him beside her. The damsel glanced up dismayed, and her whole shape trembled over the brink. Richard sprang from his boat into the water. Pressing a hand beneath her foot, which she had thrust against the crumbling wet sides of the bank to save herself, he enabled her to recover her balance, and gain safe earth, whither he followed her.